Yes, Women Can Be Narcissists Too

Graham McFarland

Copyright Notice

Copyright © 2025 by Graham "Gmac" McFarland. All rights reserved.

No part of this publication may be reproduced, distributed, or transmitted in any form or by any means, including photocopying, recording, or other electronic or mechanical methods, without the prior written permission of the copyright owner, except in the case of brief quotations embodied in critical reviews and certain other non-commercial uses permitted by copyright law.

For permission requests, write to the publisher

ISBN Number eBook: 978-1-7638393-5-9
ISBN Number Printed: 978-1-7638393-4-2
ISBN Number Hard Cover: 978-1-7638393-6-6
ISBN Number Kindle : 978-1-7638393-7-3

Disclaimer

"The information in this book is for informational purposes only and does not constitute legal, financial, or professional advice."

Acknowledgments for Trademarks

"All brand names and product names used in this book are trademarks, registered trademarks, or trade names of their respective holders."

CONTENTS

	Yes, Women Can Be Narcissists Too	1
1	Is there a Narcissism Epidemic	9
2	Tactics of Narcissistic Behavior	17
3	Stereotyped as a Man	29
4	Recognizing Narcissistic Traits in Women	34
5	Further Identifying Female Narcissists	41
6	Strategies for Male Victims to Overcome Abuse	59
7	Finding Your Future	70
8	Action Plan	78
9	INDUSTRY Experts to look out for	89
10	The Power of Your Journey	98
11	Why I wrote this book	106
	One of my favorite books	109
	Top Books About NARCISSISM	111

Yes, Women Can Be Narcissists Too

For the last twenty years, I lived through something I could never have imagined—something that society told me didn't, or couldn't, exist. I was in relationships with not just one, but two narcissistic partners.

And for two decades, I experienced the slow erosion of my confidence, my sense of self, and my belief in love and trust. What makes this journey even more painful is the reaction I received whenever I tried to speak about it.

Whenever I opened up to friends, family, or even professionals, I was met with disbelief, skepticism, or outright dismissal. The narrative that "women can't be narcissists" was so deeply ingrained in the collective psyche that my experiences were brushed aside. People told me I was overreacting, that all relationships have ups and downs, or worse, that I was simply misunderstanding my partners.

This lack of validation not only deepened my sense of isolation but also forced me to question my own reality.

I found myself trapped in a cycle of confusion and self-doubt. My partners were master manipulators, experts in emotional control, and architects of elaborate facades that made them appear caring, kind, and selfless to the outside world. Behind closed doors, however, it was a different story—one filled with control, silent treatment, emotional blackmail, and an unrelenting quest to undermine my self-worth. I was walking on eggshells, never knowing what would set off the next storm of accusations, guilt-trips, or cold detachment.

The first narcissistic partner I encountered presented herself as the perfect woman—charming, intelligent, and compassionate. She swept me off my feet with her charisma and seemingly endless love.

But over time, the mask she wore began to slip off. Small criticisms became daily occurrences, my successes were diminished, and my failures magnified. It was taboo for me to celebrate any of my wins in life, as they were not hers.

She isolated me from my support network, my awesome mates. Before I knew it, I was caught in a web of control, feeling as though I was always one step away from disappointing her. As our relationship deteriorated, I discovered her growing dependence on alcohol, her infidelity, and her tendency to engage in domestic violence when things didn't go her way.

Her need for constant validation led her to seek attention from others, and eventually, she crossed the line into full-blown cheating. I found myself questioning everything—was it my fault? Had I driven her to it? But no amount of love or sacrifice could have changed her.

*"manipulation doesn't
always look
like what you think"*

Graham McFarland

When I finally gathered the courage to leave, I thought I had learned my lesson. I believed I could recognize the signs of narcissistic abuse and never fall into the same trap again. I later learned that most narcissists have a way of sensing my vulnerability, and I found myself in another toxic relationship, with patterns so eerily familiar that it was like reliving the same nightmare.

The second relationship was filled with red flags from the start—flirting with other men, most of her best friends were male, and they were open about how they felt about her. She had suspicious secrecy with her phone, and an obsession with social media validation, often just posts about her, even if it was an experience that I was a part of, I was not in the post.

But you know it, I kept putting up with it because she had me convinced that I was the problem. Every time I questioned her of her behaviour, she skilfully turned the around, making me doubt myself and my insecurities. I at the time did not consider myself as insecure, that's the strange part to all of this.

She insisted her interactions with other men were harmless, that I was too controlling or jealous. I tried harder to be the perfect partner, to trust her, to do whatever it took to make the relationship work. But behind my back, she was engaging in secret online relationships, emotionally investing in other men while making me feel like I was being paranoid.

Despite the mounting evidence, I couldn't let go. I was stuck in the cycle of her constant reassurance followed by betrayal. I lived in fear of losing her, believing that maybe if I changed myself, she would stop looking elsewhere. I had been at the end of a relationship before, I didn't want to be a failure again.

But it took me years to realize that I was chasing an illusion—she was never going to change because the problem was never me; it was always her insatiable need for attention and validation, it was every day.

What made these relationships particularly difficult was the societal belief that narcissism is a predominantly male trait. We've all heard about the "narcissistic man"—the domineering, egotistical, self-centred type. But when it comes to women, there is little awareness, and even less support. The general response I received was that women are naturally more nurturing, caring, and emotionally intelligent. How could they possibly be narcissistic?

This blind spot in society's understanding of narcissism left me in a place of profound isolation. Seeking help from professionals often resulted in further frustration. Counsellors and therapists were often quick to attribute my struggles to my own shortcomings or communication issues, rarely entertaining the idea that my partners' behaviour was calculated, manipulative, and destructive.

I remember one counsellor using words like "male chauvinist", that a "woman's life isn't just cooking meals and washing clothes". The irony at the time, is that I was the main cook of the house and washed my own clothes, even offering most days to do hers. We both worked full time. You have to remember I was brought up by a single mother, who was raising 6 children and worked fulltime. But that's how I was portrayed to the counsellor, and in their ignorance never explored what home life really was for us.

Friends and family, despite their best intentions, advised me to be patient, to communicate better, or to try and "understand her side." Each time I heard these words, it felt like another blow to my already fragile sense of self. "understand her side… understand her side….."..

It wasn't until I stumbled upon the term "female narcissist" in my own research that everything started making sense, mind you that it was well after these relationships had failed.

I began reading stories of others who had endured similar relationships, and for the first time, I realized that I was not alone.

The behaviour's I had endured had names—**gaslighting, triangulation, love-bombing, devaluation, and discard**. More importantly, I learned that narcissism does not discriminate by gender. Women, just like men, can display these traits and cause significant harm to their partners, families, and colleagues.

Writing this book is my way of breaking the silence. For years, I lived in my shame and confusion, believing that I was the problem, that I wasn't enough, or that I was simply "too sensitive." But now I understand the truth, and I want others to see it too. This book is for the countless men, and daughters of narcissistic woman, who have been dismissed, ridiculed, or ignored when they tried to share their experiences. It is for those who are currently in relationships that feel suffocating and toxic but can't quite pinpoint why. It is for those who are trying to piece themselves back together after walking away from a narcissistic woman and struggling to find validation in their pain.

I want this book to be your source of hope. It is possible to recognize the red flags, to set boundaries, and to reclaim your life from the grip of narcissistic abuse. There is a way forward, and healing is not just possible—it is inevitable with the right knowledge, support, and determination.

By sharing my story, I hope to validate the experiences of others and encourage open discussions about the reality of female narcissists. It's time to challenge the stereotypes and start acknowledging that narcissism knows no gender. Whether you are a man reading this book in search of answers, the child of a controlling mother, a friend or family member trying to support someone affected by narcissistic abuse, or even the common sceptic questioning if this phenomenon is real—I invite you to read with an open mind and heart.

My journey through these relationships has been very painful for me, but it has also been enlightening. If this book can help even one person find clarity, strength, and freedom from narcissistic abuse, then my struggles will have been worth it.

Together, we can break the stigma, create awareness, and support those who have suffered in silence for far too long.

*"You are not alone.
you are not imagining it.
and most importantly, you are not powerless"*

Graham McFarland

1

Is there a Narcissism Epidemic

In recent years, psychologists and social commentators have raised concerns about what has been termed the "narcissism epidemic," suggesting that contemporary society is experiencing a significant rise in narcissistic traits and behaviours.

This concept, popularized by researchers such as Jean M. Twenge and W. Keith Campbell (*in their book The Narcissism Epidemic: Living in the Age of Entitlement*), argues that cultural and societal changes over the past few decades have contributed to an increase in narcissism, particularly in Western societies.

The argument draws upon factors such as social media, changing parenting styles, and shifts in cultural values have created an environment that fosters self-absorption, entitlement, and an exaggerated focus on self-image.

With my desire to understand firstly my last 2 decades of relationships, and the exploration of this concept to help others, I have come across a few theories that professionals are now "finally" shifting the narrative to better understand narcissistic behaviour.

So please be patient as I share what I have learned from these academics, and hopefully we can start to work on some exercises and practices to help you understand and act.

Theoretical Foundations of the Narcissism Epidemic

The idea of a narcissism epidemic is rooted in psychological theories that suggest personality traits can be influenced by cultural and environmental factors.

Traditionally, narcissism has been understood as a stable personality trait that exists on a spectrum, with extreme manifestations classified as:

"Narcissistic Personality Disorder" (NPD).

However, the epidemic suggests that broader social trends are fostering an increase in subclinical narcissism—traits that do not meet the criteria for NPD but still lead to self-centred behaviour's that can negatively impact relationships and society. For me this explained a lot of my experiences.

One key argument supporting the epidemic theory is the shift from collectivist to individualistic cultural values in many parts of the world, particularly in the West, and particularly in my hometown of Sydney Australia.

Societies that prioritize individual achievement, personal success, and self-expression over communal well-being and social harmony are more likely to encourage narcissistic tendencies.

This shift is reflected in various aspects of life today, from the rise of influencer culture to the increasing focus on personal branding and self-promotion.

Evidence Supporting the Narcissism Epidemic

Empirical Studies on Rising Narcissism Levels

A different approach to research has suggested that narcissistic traits have been increasing over the past few decades.

Studies using the "Narcissistic Personality Inventory" (NPI), a widely used measure of narcissistic traits, have found that scores among college students in the United States have steadily increased since the 1980s.

When reading "Twenge and Campbell's" research they found that young adults today report higher levels of narcissism compared to previous generations, often exhibiting traits such as entitlement, vanity, and an inflated sense of self-importance.

Does this sound familiar???

Social Media and the Cultivation of Narcissistic Traits

One of the most cited factors in the rise of narcissism is the advent and proliferation of social media platforms. Platforms such as Instagram, TikTok, and Facebook encourage users to curate and present idealized versions of themselves, leading to an emphasis on external validation through likes, comments, and followers.

Studies have shown that excessive social media use correlates with higher levels of narcissistic traits, as individuals become increasingly focused on appearance, status, and personal branding. Social media also fosters a culture of comparison, where individuals measure their self-worth based on their online presence rather than intrinsic qualities.

Parenting Styles and Self-Esteem Movements

Changes in parenting practices over the past few decades have also been linked to rising narcissism. For me, especially in a blended family, I now see how this was evident.

The self-esteem movement, which gained traction in the 1980s and 1990s, encouraged parents and educators to prioritize boosting children's self-worth, often without reinforcing the value of hard work, humility, and resilience.

As a result, some psychologists argue that children raised with an excessive focus on self-esteem may develop a sense of entitlement and a distorted sense of their abilities.

Helicopter parenting and overpraising can contribute to narcissistic tendencies by shielding children from failure and teaching them that they are inherently special. And now those teenagers are having children breeding another level of concern.

Consumer Culture and Materialism

Today's consumer culture plays a significant role in reinforcing narcissistic values. Advertising and marketing strategies often promote messages of self-indulgence, personal success, and the pursuit of perfection.

The emphasis on luxury goods, personal enhancement, and status symbols contributes to a culture where self-worth is closely tied to external achievements and possessions.

Research has found that individuals who place a high value on materialism and external validation are more likely to exhibit narcissistic tendencies.

Reality Television and Celebrity Culture

The rise of reality television and celebrity culture has further normalized narcissistic behaviour. I absolutely dread these reality shows, its so painful watching these people.

These shows emphasize competition, self-promotion, and dramatic personal conflicts often glorify individuals who exhibit narcissistic traits. The constant exposure to celebrity lifestyles and influencer culture can lead individuals to adopt similar behaviour's, striving for attention and validation in their own lives.

*"narcissism has
no gender."*

Graham McFarland

Criticisms and Counterarguments

While there is substantial evidence to suggest that narcissistic behaviours are becoming more prevalent, some researchers argue that the concept of a narcissism epidemic is overstated.

Some critics point out that increased self-expression and confidence should not automatically be equated with pathological narcissism. Additionally, they argue that measures of narcissism, such as the NPI, may be capturing cultural changes rather than clinical narcissism.

Some research suggests that while grandiose narcissism (characterized by overt arrogance and attention-seeking) may be more visible, vulnerable narcissism (characterized by insecurity and hypersensitivity to criticism) may also be on the rise, indicating a more complex picture of societal trends.

Yes... that's right, like a reverse style that I encountered, often hidden within relationships, but it's there in todays society. And it's the nature of this book to explore the new research identifying...
"Vulnerable Narcissism".

So, what does this all mean?

The concept of a narcissism epidemic highlights important cultural and psychological trends that have shaped modern society.

While evidence suggests an increase in narcissistic traits due to factors such as social media, parenting styles, and cultural shifts, it is essential to distinguish between healthy self-esteem and harmful narcissism.

Recognizing the social factors contributing to narcissistic behaviours can help individuals and policymakers take steps to foster healthier values, emphasizing empathy, resilience, and authentic connections in an increasingly individualistic world.

2

Tactics of Narcissistic Behavior

Learning to Identify the Manipulation

Narcissistic behavior thrives in subtlety, manipulation, and control. Oh boy can they be subtle…

Often, the tactics used by narcissists are so ingrained in their interactions that victims don't realize they are being manipulated until the damage has already been done. Understanding these tactics is essential to breaking free from their grip.

This is your guide to identifying and understanding the most common narcissistic behavior's, their variations, and their severity, so you can stop, listen, and learn to protect yourself from further harm.

Agreed Narcissistic Behaviors:
"Gas-lighting,
Love-Bombing,
Triangulation,
Silent Treatment,
Blame-Shifting,
Projection,
Hoovers and False Apologies,
Devaluation and Discard"

Gaslighting

The agreed definition:
Gaslighting is a psychological tactic where the narcissist manipulates you into questioning your reality, memories, or perceptions. This tactic allows them to maintain control by making you doubt yourself.

Variations and Severity

Subtle Gaslighting:
Simple phrases like, "That never happened," or "You're overreacting," used to dismiss your feelings or experiences.

Severe Gaslighting:
More elaborate lies that rewrite past events, often convincing you that your memory is faulty. This can escalate to making you believe you're mentally unstable.

Here is an example from my past:
You confront a narcissist about something hurtful they said, and their response is, "I never said that. You're imagining things," leaving you second-guessing your memory.

How I should have responded:
Keep a journal of incidents to validate your reality. Respond calmly with, "I remember it differently, and my feelings are valid." Seek outside perspectives from trusted friends or professionals.

Love-Bombing

The agreed definition:
Love-bombing is the narcissist's tactic of overwhelming you with affection, attention, and compliments to gain your trust and dependence early in the relationship. And also, after that moment when they went way too far destroying you.

Variations and Severity

Mild Love-Bombing:
Excessive compliments or constant communication, making you feel like the most important person in their world.

Severe Love-Bombing:
Lavish gifts, promises of a perfect future, and public declarations of affection designed to create an emotional dependency.

Here is an example from my experiences:
Early in the relationship, they text you constantly, shower you with gifts, and talk about marriage or a dream future within weeks of meeting. Isn't this normal? Right?

How I should have responded:
Be cautious if the relationship progresses too quickly. Ask yourself if their actions align with their words over time. Set boundaries for emotional and physical pacing.

Triangulation

The agreed definition:
Triangulation involves the narcissist bringing a third party into the dynamic to manipulate or control the victim. They may use this tactic to create jealousy, stir conflict, or gain leverage. This would happen almost all the time for me, especially within the vulnerable narcissism world.

Variations and Severity

Mild Triangulation:
Subtle comparisons, such as, "Why can't you be more like [third party]?"

Severe Triangulation: Actively pitting people against each other by spreading lies or playing favourites.

Here is an example from my experience:
They might say, "My ex used to do this for me, and it made me feel so special," to make you feel insecure.

How to Respond:
Avoid engaging in comparisons or conflict.

Assert your boundaries by stating, "I won't be compared to others in this way." Recognize the tactic as a form of manipulation and disengage.

Silent Treatment

Here is the agreed definition:
The silent treatment is used by narcissists to punish you or regain control after a disagreement by withdrawing communication or attention.

Variations and Severity

Passive Silent Treatment:
Ignoring calls, texts, or questions for hours or days.

Aggressive Silent Treatment:
Physically isolating themselves while making it clear their silence is intentional and meant to hurt you.

Here is an example from my past:
After a minor disagreement, they stop responding to your messages or pretend you don't exist, forcing you to beg for reconciliation.

How to Respond:
Refuse to chase their attention. Address the behaviour calmly by saying, "If you're upset, we can talk, but I won't engage in silent treatment." Give them space but focus on maintaining your emotional stability.

Blame-Shifting

Here is the agreed definition:
Blame-shifting is when the narcissist avoids accountability by blaming you or others for their mistakes or actions.

Variations and Severity

Mild Blame-Shifting:
"If you hadn't done that, I wouldn't have reacted this way."

Severe Blame-Shifting:
Completely denying responsibility for their actions, even when confronted with evidence.

Here is an example from my past:
They hurt your feelings, but when you confront them, they say, "This is your fault for being so sensitive," making you feel like the problem.

How to Respond:
Don't accept responsibility for their actions.
Use statements like, "Your actions are your choice, and I'm not responsible for them." Focus on setting boundaries rather than arguing.

TACTICS OF NARCISSISTIC BEHAVIOR

*"manipulation feels like love,
until it doesn't."*

Graham McFarland

Projection

Here is the agreed definition:
Projection occurs when the narcissist accuses you of behaviors or intentions, they are guilty of themselves.

Variations and Severity

Mild Projection:
Accusing you of being selfish when they are the ones acting selfishly.

Severe Projection:
Accusing you of cheating or dishonesty when they are the ones engaging in those behaviors. And.... This was a common event in my past, later proven which led to the final demise of the relationship between us.

Here is an example from my past:
They accuse you of lying or being untrustworthy while they're the ones withholding the truth.

How to Respond:
Stay grounded in your truth. Respond with, "I'm not responsible for how you perceive me; I know my intentions."
Avoid falling into defensive arguments.

Hoovers and False Apologies

Here is the agreed definition:

Narcissists use "hoovering" to suck you back into their control after you've distanced yourself, often through fake apologies or grand gestures. Just a note the slang "Hoovering, comes from the carpet vacuum cleaner brand "Hoover". A hoover sucks up the dust from your carpet.

Variations and Severity

Subtle Hoovering:

A random message saying, "I miss you," or "I've been thinking about you."

Severe Hoovering:

Over-the-top apologies, gifts, or promises of change that never materialize.

Here is an example I witnessed:

After a breakup, they show up unannounced with flowers, promising they've changed, only to revert to old behaviours once you let them back in.

How to Respond:

Recognize the pattern and avoid getting pulled back in. Block or limit communication if necessary. Focus on why you left in the first place.

Devaluation and Discard

Here is the agreed definition:
The narcissist initially idealizes you, then gradually devalues you before ultimately discarding you, often abruptly and cruelly.

Variations and Severity

Mild Devaluation:
Small, hurtful comments like, "You're not as interesting as you used to be."

Severe Discard:
Abruptly ending the relationship without explanation, often while moving on to someone else. In my cases they had overlapped the relationships before discarding me.

Here is an example from my experience:
After months of criticizing you, they suddenly end things, leaving you with no closure while flaunting a new relationship online.

How to Respond:
Accept that their actions are a reflection of their behaviour, not your worth. Avoid seeking closure
from them—it will only reopen wounds. I never learned this one at all. Seek therapy or support to process the experience and heal.

So, what does this all mean?

The tactics used by narcissists are designed to confuse, control, and manipulate. They come in many forms and vary in severity, but their goal is always the same: to maintain power over you.

They may not use all of these behaviors, but by learning to recognize these behaviors, you take the first step toward breaking free from their hold.

Remember,
Knowledge is power.

The more you understand these tactics, the better equipped you'll be to protect yourself, set boundaries, and ultimately build a life free from manipulation.

You don't have to live under their control. Stop, listen, and learn—your freedom starts here.

*"social media
is a narcissist's
playground."*

Graham McFarland

3

Stereotyped as a Man

So, narcissism, is characterized by traits such as grandiosity, entitlement, and a lack of empathy, has often been stereo typically associated with men.

This perception is rooted in societal norms and historical contexts that have traditionally linked assertiveness and dominance, traits commonly observed in narcissistic behavior, to masculinity.

Consequently, narcissism in women has been less recognized or is often misinterpreted, leading to a gender bias in both clinical settings and the understanding in the community too.

Over the past years I have read a lot of research, research that has explored the prevalence and expression of narcissistic traits across genders.

"A meta-analytic review" by "Grijalva, E., Newman, D. A., Tay, L., Donnellan, M. B., Harms, P. D., Robins, R. W., & Yan, T. (2015)"
analyzed data spanning 31 years and found that men consistently scored higher than women on the Narcissistic Personality Inventory (NPI). The study identified significant gender differences in the facets of Leadership/Authority and Exploitative/Entitlement, with men scoring higher in these areas.

But the difference in the Grandiose/Exhibitionism facet was minimal. The authors suggest that these disparities may be influenced by societal expectations and gender roles that encourage assertiveness and authority in men while discouraging such traits in women.

The "Diagnostic and Statistical Manual of Mental Disorders", known as (DSM-5), reports that up to 75% of individuals diagnosed with Narcissistic Personality Disorder (NPD) are male.

This statistic may reflect a clinical bias, where narcissistic traits in women are under-diagnosed or misdiagnosed. Remember my experience of "vulnerable narcissism" in my past.

Women exhibiting narcissistic behaviours may be more likely to receive diagnoses such as Borderline Personality Disorder (BPD), especially when their narcissism presents in vulnerable forms characterized by hypersensitivity and insecurity. This misclassification underscores the need for a more nuanced understanding of how narcissism manifests differently across genders.

While grandiose narcissism—marked by overt arrogance and dominance—is more commonly associated with men, women are more likely to exhibit **vulnerable narcissism.**

This form is characterized by defensiveness, sensitivity to criticism, and a fragile self-esteem. These traits can be less conspicuous, leading to under recognition in both clinical practice and societal contexts.

A study highlighted by "City University of London" found that men scored higher on grandiose narcissism, whereas women scored higher on vulnerable narcissism, suggesting distinct gender-based expression of narcissistic traits.

Societal norms play a significant role in shaping the expression and perception of narcissism. Traditional gender roles often promote assertiveness and self-promotion in men, while encouraging modesty and relational focus in women.

These expectations can lead to the underreporting or misinterpretation of narcissistic traits in women. Jeffrey Kluger, in his book "The Narcissist Next Door," suggests that patriarchal societies are more likely to tolerate and even expect narcissistic behaviours in men, while similar behaviours in women are often criticized or pathologized differently.

The gendered perceptions of narcissism have significant implications for diagnosis and treatment. What I have been focusing on over the past few years, is to have everyone become aware of potential biases and consider how narcissistic traits may manifest differently in men and women.

A nuanced approach that accounts for these differences is essential for accurate diagnosis and effective intervention. Further research is needed to develop gender-sensitive diagnostic criteria and therapeutic strategies that address the unique presentations of narcissism across genders.

Again, what does all this mean?

The prevailing view of narcissism as predominantly a male phenomenon is a result of both societal biases and historical diagnostic practices.

Evidence indicates that while men may exhibit higher levels of certain narcissistic traits, women also display narcissism, often in less overt forms.

Recognizing and understanding these gender differences is crucial for accurate diagnosis, effective treatment, and the dismantling of stereotypes that hinder our comprehension of narcissistic personality disorder.

Here are some references I have read that built my point of view on Vulnerable Narcissism:

GENDER DIFFERENCES IN NARCISSISM: A meta-analytic review. Psychological Bulletin, 141(2), 261–310.
Grijalva, E., Newman, D. A., Tay, L., Donnellan, M. B., Harms, P. D., Robins, R. W., & Yan, T. (2015).

DIAGNOSTIC AND STATISTICAL MANUAL OF MENTAL DISORDERS (5th ed.).
American Psychiatric Association. (2013). Arlington, VA: American Psychiatric Publishing.

NARCISSISM: WHY IT'S LESS OBVIOUS IN WOMEN THAN IN MEN – but can be just as dangerous. City University of London. (2024, June).

THE NARCISSIST NEXT DOOR: understanding the monster in your family, in your office, in your bed—in your world Kluger, J. (2014).. Riverhead Books.

ISSUES IN THE ASSESSMENT OF NARCISSISTIC PERSONALITY DISORDER: Shedding Light On The Dsm–5 Approach To Narcissism. Personality Disorders: Theory, Research, And Treatment, 9(2), 103–108.Wright, A. G. C., & Edershile, E. A. (2018).

*"Evidence indicates
that while men may exhibit higher levels of certain narcissistic
traits,*

*women
also display narcissism, often in less overt forms called,
<u>vulnerable narcissism.</u>"*

Graham McFarland

Recognizing Narcissistic Traits in Women

When most people think of narcissism, they often picture the stereotypical traits commonly associated with men—dominance, arrogance, and an inflated sense of self-worth.

However, female narcissists exist and can exhibit equally damaging behaviours, albeit in often more covert and emotionally manipulative ways. Understanding the unique traits of female narcissists is crucial for men who may find themselves in relationships—whether personal or professional—where they feel manipulated, devalued, and emotionally drained.

Excessive Need for Admiration

All female narcissists have an insatiable need for admiration and validation from those around them. They may go to great lengths to ensure they are constantly in the spotlight, using their charm, beauty, or social skills to command attention.

This often manifests in behaviours such as posting attention-seeking content on social media, dominating conversations with tales of their accomplishments, or fishing for compliments.

An example I would like to share:

In a romantic relationship, a female narcissist might constantly seek affirmation from her partner, demanding reassurance about her attractiveness or intelligence. Any perceived lack of attention can lead to sulking, passive-aggressive behaviour, or even dramatic threats to leave the relationship.

Manipulative Behaviour

Unlike the overt dominance commonly observed in male narcissists, female narcissists often employ subtle, manipulative tactics to control those around them. They might present themselves as victims to garner sympathy or use guilt and emotional blackmail to get their way.

Another example I had in my time:

A female narcissistic boss might play favourites, offering praise and recognition only when it serves her agenda while subtly undermining colleagues she sees as threats. She might make promises she never intends to keep or manipulate others into doing her work under the guise of teamwork. I have worked for many amazing woman leaders in my career, in fact most of my managers have been woman, but there were a few that fit this mould!

Preoccupation with Appearance

Female narcissists tend to be excessively focused on their looks and public image, often using their appearance as a tool to influence and manipulate others. They invest heavily in their physical presentation and may use their attractiveness to climb social or professional ladders.

A common example:

In social settings, a female narcissist may spend hours curating her online presence to project a life of perfection, concealing any aspects that don't fit her carefully crafted persona. She may judge others harshly based on their looks and social status.

Envy and Competitiveness

A notable trait of female narcissists is their deep-seated envy and competitiveness. They are often unable to celebrate others' successes and may resort to underhanded tactics to diminish their rivals.

This can manifest in professional environments where they undermine colleagues or in friendships where they downplay others' achievements.

An example would be:
A female narcissistic friend might constantly "one-up" stories or subtly criticize accomplishments, positioning herself as superior while dismissing the achievements of others.

Identifying Female Narcissists in Various Contexts

Identifying a female narcissist can be challenging, as their behaviour often flies under the radar, masked by charm and social finesse. But recognizing key patterns in different environments, men can learn to identify narcissistic individuals and protect themselves from emotional manipulation and abuse.

In Personal Relationships

In intimate relationships, a female narcissist can be charming and affectionate at first, making her partner feel like the centre of her world. But over time, this affection often turns into a form of control.

She may use love-bombing to gain control, followed by emotional withdrawal to manipulate her partner's behaviour.

Signs to watch for:

1. Constant need for praise and validation.
2. Jealousy and possessiveness disguised as concern.
3. Gaslighting tactics that make the partner question their reality.
4. Frequent emotional outbursts when things don't go her way.

An example here is:
A man in a relationship with a female narcissist might find himself constantly apologizing, even when he's done nothing wrong, as she shifts blame and manipulates him into feeling guilty.

> "she's not
> 'too good to be true...'
> she's a narcissist."
>
> Graham McFarland

In the Workplace

Female narcissists in the workplace often present themselves as highly competent and ambitious, but their primary goal is self-promotion at the expense of others. They thrive in environments where competition is high, and recognition is valued.

Signs to watch for:

1. Taking credit for others' work.
2. Creating drama or tension to divert attention from their shortcomings.
3. Manipulating superiors by portraying themselves as indispensable.
4. Subtly undermining colleagues through gossip and passive-aggressive tactics.

An example here would be:
An employee may find themselves continually sidelined by a female narcissistic supervisor who micromanages their work and takes credit for their ideas in meetings.

On Social Media

Social media provides a perfect platform for female narcissists to curate an idealized version of their lives. They thrive on external validation and use their online presence to manipulate perceptions.

Signs to watch for:

1. Excessive posting of selfies and achievements.
2. Fishing for compliments through vague or self-deprecating posts.
3. Engaging in online drama and seeking public validation.

An example here would be:
A narcissistic colleague might portray herself as a successful and generous leader online, while she belittles her team and creates a toxic work environment.

Relationship App's on Social Media

Relationship social media app's are a magnet for narcissism. Especially Vulnerable Narcissist's. This environment is like a paradise for them, they thrive there.

If you are on these app's:

- All of the traits are present within the conversations.
- Someone drops in and out of conversation with you, "Like they are getting bored" with you.
- Talk poorly about others they have met.
- They start framing a future that really makes you uncomfortable because you don't know them yet.
- In-authentic self-presentation, like a photo from 10 years ago.

And sometimes... you might find out that your current partner still has the app on there phone, or an active account. A friend who has been recently made single, might find your partners profile active on these platforms, true story indeed.

5

Further Identifying Female Narcissists

In Various Contexts

Recognizing a female narcissist is not always straightforward. Their behaviours are often subtle, masked by charm and manipulation, making it difficult to pinpoint the toxic patterns early on.

I learned this the hard way. Over the course of two decades, I experienced their tactics in personal relationships, professional environments, and even online interactions.

This explores these contexts, helping you identify narcissistic behaviour and, more importantly, equipping you with tools to address and overcome their hold on you.

In Personal Relationships

In romantic relationships, a female narcissist may present herself as the perfect partner at first, using her charm and sexuality to draw you in. This initial phase, often referred to as "**love-bombing**," is intoxicating.

She makes you feel like the centre of her universe—complimenting you, showering you with affection, and convincing you that you've finally found someone who truly understands you. But the reality beneath the surface is far more sinister.

I'll never forget how my first partner would use jealousy as a tool to control me. She had a way of flirting with other men, both in front of me and subtly in social settings, just enough to make me feel uneasy but not enough to confront her outright. If I mentioned it, she would accuse me of being paranoid or insecure, flipping the narrative until I was the one apologizing. Over time, this constant cycle of confusion and self-doubt left me questioning my worth.

Red Flags to Look Out For:

1. Emotional Manipulation: Tears, threats, or playing the victim whenever you try to address issues in the relationship.
2. Jealousy and Control: While she flirts freely, she might accuse you of disloyalty for minor, innocent actions, like speaking to a female colleague.
3. Validation-Seeking: She constantly asks for reassurance about her looks or intelligence, demanding compliments as if they are her lifeline.

Solution:

The first step is to trust your instincts. If something feels off, it probably is. Document her behaviours and how they make you feel, even if it's just for your own clarity.

Boundaries are your greatest ally. For example, when she flirts with others, calmly and assertively state, "I feel disrespected when this happens, and I won't tolerate it."

If her behaviour doesn't change, you must consider if this is the kind of relationship you want to stay in.

Moving Past the Hold:

Understand that the problem lies in her need for validation, not in your shortcomings. Therapy can be a powerful tool to rebuild self-esteem and break free from the cycle of manipulation.

Surround yourself with supportive friends and family who can provide perspective and encouragement.

Real World Example of a Mans Experience:

One man I spoke to shared how his partner would bring up her exes during arguments, comparing him unfavourably to them. He realized this wasn't normal or healthy when a friend pointed out the emotional damage it was causing him.

He set a boundary, saying, "If you bring up your exes again, I'll have to walk away from the conversation." While she initially protested, he stuck to it, and eventually, he left the relationship when the behaviour didn't improve.

*"healing starts
with awareness."*

Graham McFarland

In the Workplace

The professional environment can be a breeding ground for female narcissists. In my career, I've encountered women who used passive-aggressive tactics, gossip, and even outright sabotage to climb the corporate ladder. But don't ever try calling it out, its career suicide.

In all the experiences I have witnessed, they eventually fall from grace. Sometimes quickly, but sadly often way too long.

These individuals often present themselves as charming and competent, gaining the trust of superiors while undermining colleagues behind the scenes.

One colleague I worked with was a classic example. She had a talent for making herself look like the hero while quietly throwing others under the bus. If a project succeeded, she would take credit, often embellishing her contributions. If something went wrong, she'd subtly shift the blame, using phrases like,
"I tried to warn him, but he wouldn't listen."

Over time, her manipulative tactics created a toxic work environment where everyone walked on eggshells.

Red Flags to Look Out For:

- Hiding Competence: She uses charm and buzzwords to mask a lack of factual knowledge or skill.
- Credit-Stealing: She takes credit for group achievements while downplaying the efforts of others.
- Gossip and Division: She spreads rumours to isolate and weaken potential competitors.

Solution:
Keep a record of your work and contributions. If she tries to claim credit for something you did, having documentation will allow you to set the record straight.

Avoid engaging in her gossip—refuse to participate in conversations where she badmouths others. Focus on building relationships with colleagues and superiors based on honesty and integrity.

Moving Past the Hold:
If her behaviour continues to create stress or damage your career, consider involving HR or seeking support from a mentor. Recognize that her actions reflect her insecurities, not your abilities. I have even moved on from companies because of this.

Real World Example:
A friend of mine dealt with a narcissistic boss who constantly micromanaged and belittled him in front of others. He began keeping a detailed log of their interactions, which he eventually used to file a complaint with HR.

While the process was challenging, it resulted in the company reassigning him to a different department, allowing him to thrive in a healthier environment. One could argue that's not right that he had to move, but to be honest, life is short, he flourished in the new team anyway.

| 47 | – FURTHER IDENTIFYING FEMALE NARCISSISTS

*"recognize
the red flags
before it's too late."*

Graham McFarland

On Social Media

Social media has become the ultimate stage for narcissists, offering endless opportunities to curate an idealized version of themselves. Female narcissists use platforms like Instagram, Facebook, and TikTok to seek validation through likes, comments, and followers.

One of my partners was obsessed with her online presence. She would spend hours editing photos, crafting the perfect captions, and monitoring her posts' engagement. Behind the scenes, she was constantly texting and messaging other men—conversations she dismissed as "harmless" but that made me feel disrespected and devalued. When I confronted her, she turned the tables, accusing me of being controlling and insecure.

Red Flags to Look Out For:

- Excessive Selfies: Posting constant images with captions designed to elicit praise and admiration.
- Materialistic Posts: Flaunting possessions or experiences to project a false image of success.
- Online Flirting: Engaging in secretive or inappropriate conversations under the guise of "harmless fun."

Solution:
It's important to set boundaries regarding social media use in the relationship. For example, agree on what's appropriate and what crosses the line. If she dismisses your concerns or accuses you of being controlling, pay attention to the pattern—it could indicate deeper issues.

To be honest, online activity like this is a MASSIVE red flag. Don't get drawn into online personalities.

Moving Past the Hold:

Remind yourself that her online behaviour is not a reflection of your worth. Focus on creating an authentic, offline life that brings you joy and fulfilment. Seek out communities of like-minded individuals who value real connections over superficial appearances.

Real World Example:

A man I spoke with discovered his partner was sending flirty messages to multiple men she met on social media. Instead of confronting her in anger, he calmly showed her the evidence and explained how it made him feel.

When she refused to take responsibility, he ended the relationship, choosing his self-respect over the illusion of love. Don't accept anything less people!

Lesser-Known Personality Indicators of Female Narcissists

While many people are familiar with the common traits of narcissists, like grandiosity, lack of empathy, and manipulation, as mentioned female narcissists often exhibit more covert and socially acceptable forms of narcissism.

When researching their behaviours I came to realise that they can be incredibly insidious, making them harder to detect as being narcissistic.

I thought I would add some lesser-known personality indicators of female narcissists that often go unnoticed in society:

Manufactured Empathy (The "Fake Caregiver")

What the "Fake Caregiver" looks like is:

Female narcissists can appear highly empathetic, often presenting themselves as caregivers, nurturers, or "fixers." They will go out of their way to help others, but not out of genuine kindness.

Instead, their generosity is transactional, it's all about control, her image, or creating debt that they will later cash in (most men will relate to this).

An example from my experience: A female narcissist may shower you with kindness and support when you're struggling, only to use it later as emotional leverage:

Have you heard this...?
"After everything I've done for you, how could you treat me like this?"

How to recognize it:
Their empathy disappears when they are not getting praise or gratitude.

They remind you constantly of what they've done for you.

They use their "kindness" as a tool for guilt-tripping.

The "Expert in Everything" Syndrome

And this is what it looks like:
Female narcissists often position themselves as the ultimate authority on any topic, especially in relationships, parenting, work, or social dynamics. They will insist they "know better" than everyone else, even if they have no real experience or knowledge. Have you come across this before?

An example to help understand this: You could be an expert in your field, but she will dismiss your knowledge and assert that she understands it better—even if she has no background in the subject.

How to recognize it:
They dismiss advice from actual professionals but demand that their own opinions be respected.
They frequently correct others, even in subjects they don't specialize in.
They gaslight you into believing you don't know as much as they do.

The "Queen of Chaos"

What it looks like when around the Queen of Chaos:

Some female narcissists create constant drama and conflict, either to keep attention on themselves or to manipulate others into taking sides. They thrive on instability because it keeps people off balance and emotionally vulnerable.

My example here is: If things are calm for too long, she might suddenly bring up an old argument, pick a fight, or create conflict with a friend or family member just to stir the pot. You will literally ask yourself... Where did this come from...

How to recognize it:
She frequently "forgets" past resolutions and reopens old wounds.
She seems emotionally bored when things are peaceful.
She pits people against each other (triangulation) and plays the victim when confronted.

The Passive-Aggressive Underminer

What the underminer looks like: Instead of direct confrontation, female narcissists often use passive-aggressive tactics to control and belittle others. This can range from subtle put-downs to backhanded compliments and disguised insults.

My example for this is: You get a promotion at work, and she says, "Wow, they must have been desperate to fill that position!". I really hated this trait.

How to recognize it:
She often makes sarcastic remarks at your expense but calls it "just a joke."
She gives compliments that don't actually feel like compliments.

She uses veiled criticism to erode your confidence over time.

The Victim Narrative Trap

What the victim trap looks like: Female narcissists often paint themselves as the victim in every situation, using their past traumas or difficult experiences as an excuse for their toxic behaviour. Always remember there is NO excuse for toxic behaviour.

My example I have witnessed here: If you try to set a boundary, she responds with, "You know I have trust issues because of my past! You should be more understanding!" And to be honest, she was eventually right with this one!

How to recognize it:
She uses her past experiences to manipulate you into compliance.
She always has a tragic backstory that justifies bad behaviour.
She refuses to take responsibility, instead blaming past traumas or other people. Never was it their fault.

The Selective Rule-Breaker

What it looks like: While most narcissists believe rules don't apply to them, female narcissists are selective about when they break them. They demand that others follow societal norms, etiquette, or house rules, except when it inconveniences them. They really believe when they break a rule, they are not!

The Rule-Breaker example here is: She insists on strict punctuality for others but is always late herself. Oh boy don't make a comment and point this out!

But be careful with this one, this just might be a cultural behaviour, as Brazilians are fashionably late all the time.

How to recognize it:

She enforces high standards for others but excuses herself from them.

She expects unquestioning respect but gives none in return.

She is highly critical of others but intolerant of criticism toward herself.

The Emotional Chameleon

You will learn that female narcissists have a unique ability to adapt their personality depending on their audience. When you become aware of it, it just blows your mind as you are watching it happen, like at parties. They can be kind and generous around new acquaintances but cold and dismissive toward close family members.

An example for you: She treats you with indifference at home but is overly affectionate and charming in front of others to maintain a perfect image. And it sounds to you so fake.

How to recognize it:

She seems like a completely different person depending on the setting.

Her kindness feels performative rather than genuine.

She "turns it on" in public but is cruel or indifferent in private.

The Image-Obsessed Self-Promoter

Female narcissists are often obsessed with their social image, curating a carefully controlled persona online and in public. They use social media for validation and often present an exaggerated version of their lives.

Example: She posts about her "perfect relationship" online while emotionally neglecting her partner behind closed doors. Or you are on a magical holiday, strolling down the beach watching a sunset, and she takes a selfie and posts it, with a message like "amazing life", but you are not in the photo or apart of her story.

How to recognize it:
She obsessively posts selfies or materialistic content for external validation.
Her social media life looks vastly different from her real life.
She is highly reactive to any perceived criticism or lack of attention online.

The Control Freak in Disguise

Unlike common overt narcissists who openly demand control, female narcissists often manipulate through subtle control tactics, such as guilt, obligation, or emotional blackmail. You often hear men talking about these amongst mates, creating jokes out of it.

My example here is: She insists on making all decisions in a relationship but phrases it as "just wanting to help" or "being more organized." But really it's a control move.

How to recognize it:
She subtly pressures you into making decisions that benefit her.

She withholds affection when things don't go her way.
She guilt-trips you for asserting independence.

The Silent Saboteur

Surely you can relate and know what it looks like: Female narcissists often sabotage others in covert ways, especially in friendships or professional settings. Instead of openly attacking someone, they plant seeds of doubt, spread subtle rumours, or undermine people behind the scenes.

Example most people would recognise: She secretly tells your coworkers that you're struggling at work while pretending to support you in person.

How you would recognize it:
She frequently "warns" others about you or paints herself as the better option.
She appears helpful while subtly undermining your credibility.
She enjoys watching others fail but feigns concern.

While female narcissists may not always exhibit the same aggressive dominance as male narcissists, their manipulation tactics can be just as damaging. Their behaviours are often more covert, making them harder to detect and even harder to confront.

What to do if you recognize these signs:
Trust your instincts. If something feels off, it probably is.
Set strong boundaries. Don't allow yourself to be guilted or manipulated.
Observe their consistency. If their kindness feels performative or conditional, it likely is.

Seek outside perspective. Narcissists thrive on isolating their victims—talk to friends or a therapist for validation.

Most importantly: You don't have to tolerate manipulation, no matter how subtle or disguised it is. Recognizing these behaviours is the first step toward reclaiming your freedom and building healthier relationships.

So, what does all this mean?

Identifying female narcissists in various contexts is a critical step in protecting your mental and emotional well-being. Whether it's a romantic partner, a coworker, or someone you follow online, recognizing the red flags allows you to set boundaries and act.

The key is to remember is that you are not alone, you are not imagining it, and you are not powerless These behaviours are **not** a reflection of your worth but of the narcissist's deep-seated insecurities and need for control.

By trusting your instincts, seeking support, and prioritizing your own well-being, you can break free from their hold and move toward a healthier, happier future.

"many men,
struggle to recognize themselves
as victims,
due to societal expectations"

Graham McFarland

6

Strategies for Male Victims to Overcome Abuse

Men who find themselves entangled with female narcissists face a unique set of challenges. Societal stigmas around masculinity often discourage men from acknowledging their pain, let alone seeking help. The isolation and emotional toll can be overwhelming, but there is hope.

Breaking free from the cycle of abuse requires actionable strategies and a commitment to rebuilding one's life. This provides practical, long-term solutions to help men regain control and move toward a healthier future.

Acknowledge the Abuse

The first and most difficult step in overcoming narcissistic abuse is admitting that it's happening. Many men struggle to recognize themselves as victims due to societal expectations that they must always be strong, unshakable, and in control.

For years, I dismissed my own experiences, thinking, "This is just how relationships are" or "I should be able to handle this." But the truth is, no one—regardless of gender—deserves to be manipulated, controlled, or emotionally abused.

A mild example from my past:
Consider your partner constantly criticizes you in private but praises you in public, creating a confusing dynamic. You feel like you're the one failing them, but in reality, this is a form of emotional manipulation.

Structured Solution:

- Start Journaling: Writing down incidents of manipulation, criticism, and control can help clarify patterns of abuse. Seeing the behaviours in black and white removes the emotional fog narcissists create.
- Recognize Gaslighting: Learn to identify when your feelings are being dismissed or twisted. Phrases like, "You're overreacting," or, "You're imagining things," are classic gaslighting tactics.
- Accept That It's Not Your Fault: Abuse is never justified, and it's not a reflection of your worth. Let go of the shame society places on male victims.
- Educate Yourself: Research narcissistic behaviours and understand the tactics they use. Knowledge is the foundation of empowerment.

Long-Term Benefit:
Acknowledging the abuse allows you to regain perspective and make informed decisions. By recognizing that the problem lies with the narcissist, not with you, you can begin to break free from their manipulative grasp.

Establish Boundaries

Once you've acknowledged the abuse, the next step is setting and maintaining clear boundaries. Narcissists thrive on crossing lines and testing limits to maintain control. Without boundaries, you leave yourself open to repeated manipulation and emotional harm.

A simple example:

A man might find himself agreeing to things he doesn't want to do—like cancelling plans with friends or taking on financial burdens—because his partner guilts him into compliance.

Structured Solution:

- Define Your Boundaries: Identify what behaviours you will no longer tolerate (e.g., shouting during arguments, blaming you for her mistakes, or invading your privacy).
- Communicate Clearly: Use "I" statements to assert your needs. For example, "I feel disrespected when I'm yelled at, and I need us to discuss things calmly."
- Be Consistent: Narcissists will test your boundaries repeatedly. Stand firm, even if it feels uncomfortable at first.
- Enforce Consequences: If a boundary is crossed, follow through with the stated consequence. For instance, if she ignores your request for space, you might disengage from the conversation or leave the room.

Long-Term Benefit:

Establishing boundaries shifts the dynamic of control. It empowers you to protect your emotional and mental well-being while signaling that manipulative behavior will no longer be tolerated.

Seek Support

One of the most isolating aspects of narcissistic abuse is the feeling that no one understands what you're going through. This is compounded by the stigma men face when they admit to being victims of emotional or psychological abuse. Finding a support system is essential for healing and gaining perspective.

An example would be:
Imagine a man hesitant to tell his friends about his struggles because he fears being judged or ridiculed. He stays silent, which deepens his feelings of isolation.

Structured Solution:
Find a Support Group: Many communities and online platforms offer groups specifically for men dealing with narcissistic abuse. Sharing your story with others who've been in your shoes can be incredibly validating.

Consult a therapist: Seek out a therapist experienced in narcissistic abuse recovery. Therapy provides a safe space to process your emotions and develop coping strategies.

Confide in Trusted Friends: Open up to friends or family members who have shown understanding and compassion in the past.

Engage with Resources: Books, podcasts, and forums on narcissistic abuse can provide valuable insights and tools for recovery.

Long-Term Benefit:
Support systems remind you that you're not alone. They provide encouragement, practical advice, and a sense of community, all of which are crucial for breaking free from the narcissist's grip.

Practice Self-Care

Narcissistic abuse can leave you feeling drained, disconnected, and lost. Rebuilding your sense of self requires a commitment to self-care. This isn't about indulgence; it's about nurturing your physical, emotional, and mental health.

An often-observed example:
A man who spent years prioritizing his partner's needs over his own might not even remember what he enjoys or values.

Structured Solution:
Prioritize Your Health: Regular exercise, a balanced diet, and sufficient sleep are foundational to feeling strong and capable.

Explore Mindfulness Practices: Activities like meditation, deep breathing, and yoga can help reduce anxiety and improve focus.

Rediscover Hobbies: Reconnect with activities that bring you joy, whether it's playing music, hiking, or woodworking.

Set Goals: Create small, achievable goals to rebuild your confidence and sense of purpose.

Celebrate Progress: Acknowledge even the smallest victories, such as sticking to a boundary or speaking up for yourself.

Long-Term Benefit:

Self-care helps you rebuild your identity and regain the confidence that narcissistic abuse often erodes. It reminds you that you are deserving of happiness, fulfillment, and peace.

Rumination
Understanding and Overcoming Repetitive Thought Cycles

What is Rumination? And watch out for this phenomenon!

Rumination is a pattern of excessive, repetitive thinking, often centered around distressing thoughts or unresolved issues. While some individuals can break free from these thought loops, others find themselves trapped in a cycle that fuels emotional distress, anxiety, and even depression. In severe cases, rumination can contribute to dysfunctional behaviors and mental health disorders.

It's important to distinguish this psychological pattern from "rumination disorder," an eating disorder involving regurgitation of food. The focus here is on mental rumination—where thoughts become obsessive and self-perpetuating.

Types of Rumination

Rumination is typically categorized into two subtypes:

Reflective Rumination:
This type involves analytical thinking, where a person reviews past events to learn and problem-solve. While it can be useful for personal growth, excessive reflection can still contribute to anxiety and stress.

Brooding Rumination:
This is a more destructive form where negative thoughts cycle continuously, reinforcing feelings of sadness, self-doubt, or hopelessness. It often leads to emotional distress, mental exhaustion, and in some cases, substance abuse or depression.

Although reflective rumination can be helpful in moderation, both types can be linked to anxiety, depression, and other mental health challenges when they become excessive.

Signs of Rumination

Rumination is a key component of depression and can make it difficult to break free from negative thinking patterns. The symptoms often overlap with depression and include:
- Constantly talking or thinking about painful experiences
- Persistent sadness or emotional numbness
- Increased irritability and mood swings
- Difficulty concentrating or making decisions
- Loss of interest in daily activities
- Low energy or motivation
- Feelings of worthlessness or helplessness
- Fatigue and excessive sleeping
- Appetite changes
- Suicidal thoughts

When rumination becomes overwhelming, it can prevent effective problem-solving and make therapy less effective, trapping individuals in a cycle of distress.

Causes of Ruminating Thoughts

Rumination often stems from early life experiences, particularly negative events that shape coping mechanisms. Adolescence and young adulthood are critical periods where emotional and cognitive patterns are formed. Since mood disorders, substance abuse, and psychosis frequently emerge during these years, rumination patterns tend to solidify alongside these conditions.

Emotional intelligence plays a role in rumination.

Studies show that:

Brooding rumination is associated with lower emotional intelligence, making individuals more vulnerable to negative thought cycles and suicidal ideation.

Reflective rumination is often linked to higher emotional intelligence, allowing for better emotional processing and problem-solving.

Coping mechanisms also influence rumination styles:

Active coping (such as mindfulness, therapy, or journaling) encourages reflective rumination, reducing the risk of depression.

Passive coping (such as avoidance or substance use) leads to brooding rumination, reinforcing feelings of helplessness.

Breaking the Cycle of Rumination

Recognizing rumination is the first step toward overcoming it. Shifting from brooding to a more reflective mindset can help regain control over thought patterns. Strategies include:

Accept the thoughts
Don't try to push away obsessive thoughts but instead accept that they are automatic and not your fault.

Distract yourself

Try to shift your focus to something else, like a new activity or calling a friend. For me I took up boxing, and hit the gym when I started down this path.

Challenge your thoughts

Question the thought and see if it's accurate. For example, if you think "no one likes me", ask yourself who told you that. Reach out to a friend and ask to catch up.

Practice mindfulness

Try meditation or deep breathing to notice your thoughts without judgment. For me it was nature, bushwalking for example was my meditation.

Practice grounding techniques

Use your senses to bring yourself back to the present. For example, you can focus on how your feet feel on the ground or listen to sounds around you. I simply would water the front nd back yards in bare foot and stand on the grass.

Practice relaxation

Try progressive muscle relaxation, where you tense and release your muscles throughout your body.

Exercise

Regular physical activity can help reduce stress, improve sleep quality, and increase self-confidence.

Set aside time for worry

Set aside a period of time each day to focus on your worries and then leave the rest of the day free of them.

Write down your thoughts

Writing down your thoughts can help you identify how repetitive they are. This is extremely helpful at night, when you are trying to sleep. Have a journal on your beside table and write these thoughts down.

Seek professional help

If these thoughts make daily life hard, a therapist can provide support and ways to cope.

My Thoughts

Overcoming narcissistic abuse is a journey that requires strength, perseverance, and self-compassion. By acknowledging the abuse, setting boundaries, seeking support, and prioritizing self-care, you can break free from the cycle of manipulation and rebuild a life filled with confidence and joy.

This journey isn't easy, but it is possible. Each step you take is a step toward reclaiming your power and rediscovering the person you were before the abuse. Seeking professional help and educating oneself about narcissistic personality traits are essential steps towards healing and building healthier relationships in the future.

STRATEGIES FOR MALE VICTIMS TO OVERCOME ABUSE

"remember:
you are not alone.
you are not imagining it.
and most importantly,
you are not powerless"

Graham McFarland

7

Finding Your Future

Surprising Yourself Beyond Narcissistic Control

When you're living under the control of a narcissist, your world shrinks. Your dreams, your goals, and even your sense of self feel impossibly distant. You lose sight of who you are, and the idea of a better future seems like a fantasy.

I know this because I lived it. For years, I couldn't see beyond the chaos and manipulation. And even if I tried to picture life without the narcissist's hold, fear would creep in:

What if life without them is worse?
What if I fail on my own?
What if I am not enough?

But here's the truth, and it's one of the hardest truths for victims to believe while they're still in the fog: life beyond the world of narcissistic control is amazing. It is more fulfilling, expansive, and joyful than you can imagine while you are trapped in their grip. And the first step to finding that future is to believe that it is possible.

The Fear of Letting Go

When you're in the thick of a narcissistic relationship, letting go feels like stepping off a cliff. Narcissists are masters at making you believe you can't survive without them. They make you feel dependent, small, and incapable. I remember the exact thoughts that kept me stuck for so long: What if I'm alone forever? What if no one ever loves me again? What if my life falls apart without them?

These fears are normal. They are the result of years of manipulation and self-doubt planted by the narcissist. But they are not the truth. The truth is, letting go is the beginning of freedom. It's the moment you reclaim your life and start moving toward the future you deserve.

"fear of life without a narcissist is temporary, but the joy of life beyond them is limitless".

Graham McFarland

The Moment Life Starts to Expand

When I finally broke free, it wasn't an instant transformation. The early days were messy, filled with doubt and moments of grief. But then something incredible happened: little by little, my world began to expand.

I started making decisions for myself again, rediscovering what I enjoyed and what made me feel alive. I began building a life that wasn't dictated by someone else's needs or manipulations. And as I embraced this freedom, opportunities I never thought possible started appearing.

In my own journey, I surprised myself in ways I could never have imagined. I ran for federal parliament, something that would have been unthinkable while I was under the narcissist's control. I built a small business, joined the board of an international company, and even learned new languages. I travelled the world, became a grandfather, and formed deep, meaningful relationships with my adult children—something that once felt like a distant dream.

And here I am now, writing and publishing books. The very fact that you're reading this is proof of how far life can take you when you're no longer living under someone else's shadow.

Lesson Learned: The life you deserve isn't just waiting for you—it's yours to create.

The Power of Knowledge

Breaking free from narcissistic control requires more than just physical distance; it requires a deep understanding of what you've experienced and why it happened. For me, educating myself about narcissism was a turning point. I devoured books, listened to experts, and connected with others who had lived through similar experiences.

Understanding narcissistic behaviour gave me clarity. I could finally see the patterns—the gaslighting, the manipulation, the emotional abuse—that had kept me trapped. This knowledge didn't just help me heal; it empowered me to build stronger boundaries and recognize toxic behaviours in the future.

Why Knowledge Matters

"Clarity, Validation, and Empowerment"

Clarity: It helps you understand that their behaviour was never about you, it was about their own insecurities and need for control.

Validation: You realize you are not alone, and your experiences are real.

Empowerment: You learn how to protect yourself from falling into similar patterns again.

My advice

Invest time in learning about narcissism. Read books, attend therapy, join support groups, and connect with others who understand. The more you know, the stronger and more confident you will become.

I have a paragraph later in the book that will suggest some books you might be interesting in reading.

Surprising Yourself

One of the most beautiful parts of this journey is rediscovering yourself. After years of being told you're not enough or that your dreams are unrealistic, you start to realize just how capable you are.

For me, it started small. I remember the first time I said "no" without feeling guilty. It felt revolutionary. From there, I began setting bigger goals—goals I had once dismissed as impossible.

I wanted to travel, so I did.
I wanted to own a farm, now I do!
I wanted to ride a Harley Davidson, now I do daily.

Each step forward was a reminder that my life was mine to shape, not someone else's to control.

Advice for Readers

Start With Small Wins, Dream Big, Take Action, and Inspiration

Start with Small Wins:
Say "no" to something you don't want to do. Revisit a hobby you gave up.

Dream Big:
Write down the goals you've always had but never believed you could achieve.

Take Action:
Break those goals into steps and start working toward them, one day at a time.

Inspiration:
The only limits on your future are the ones you place on yourself.

Life Beyond Narcissism

I often tell people that my life truly began when I let go of the narcissists who had controlled it for so long. Everything I've achieved since—my relationships, my career, my adventures—happened because I made the choice to prioritize myself.

But this isn't just about me. I've had the privilege of working with others who've broken free from narcissistic relationships, and their stories are just as inspiring. One man I know became a mentor to young men in his community, teaching them about healthy relationships. Another started his own business, something he'd always dreamed of but never believed he could do.

These stories are proof that life beyond narcissism isn't just about survival—it's about thriving. It's about creating a life so full, so joyful, and so authentic that you barely recognize the person you were when you were under the narcissist's control.

Final Thoughts: Reclaiming Your Destiny

The hardest part of leaving a narcissist is believing that life can be better without them. But I'm here to tell you, not only is it better—**it's extraordinary**.

Your future is yours to create. The control, the manipulation, the fear—they don't define you. You are stronger than you realize, and the life you've always dreamed of is waiting for you on the other side.

Start small, start to educate yourself, and take bold steps toward the life you deserve. One day, you'll look back and be amazed at how far you've come. You'll surprise yourself in ways you never thought possible. I know because I do this every day!

And you'll finally know:

You Are Not Alone.
You Are Not Imagining It.
And Most Importantly,
You Are Not Powerless.

8

Action Plan

Overcoming Narcissistic Relationships and Rebuilding Your Life

Here I want to provide a structured approach for individuals affected by narcissistic relationships to recognize, address, and move forward with confidence and self-empowerment.

This action plan is designed to help readers identify toxic behaviours, establish boundaries, seek support, and regain control of their emotional and psychological well-being.

Action 1: Recognize and Acknowledge the Abuse
Action 2: Establish Boundaries
Action 3: Limit or Cut Off Contact
Action 4: Seek Professional Support
Action 5: Rebuild Your Self-Esteem and Self-Identity
Action 6: Develop Coping Strategies for Emotional Triggers
Action 7: Create a New Vision for Your Future
Action 8: Educate Yourself to Prevent Future Toxic Relationships

Action 1:

Recognize and Acknowledge the Abuse

Steps to Take:

- Educate yourself on narcissistic behaviours and red flags (e.g., gaslighting, manipulation, love-bombing, and emotional abuse).
- Document patterns of behaviour that make you feel manipulated or controlled.
- Reflect on how the relationship has impacted your self-esteem, mental health, and well-being.
- Acknowledge that narcissistic abuse is real and that you deserve better treatment.

What you are going to achieve:

By recognizing the signs of narcissistic abuse, you empower yourself to break free from denial and take the first step toward healing. Knowledge is power / understanding what you are dealing with helps build resilience and fosters self-awareness.

Action 2:

Establish Boundaries

Steps to Take:

- Identify areas where you feel exploited or manipulated, such as emotional, financial, or social boundaries.
- Set firm, clear limits on what behaviour you will and will not tolerate (e.g., "I will not engage in arguments fuelled by blame and guilt").
- Communicate your boundaries assertively and consistently.
- Practice saying "no" without guilt and disengage from toxic interactions.
- Stay committed to your boundaries, even when met with resistance.

What you are going to achieve:

Setting boundaries protects your mental and emotional space from further harm. It reinforces your self-worth and discourages further manipulation from the narcissist.

Action 3:

Limit or Cut Off Contact

This is my main "Golden Nugget" that I tell everyone...

Steps to Take:

- Assess whether cutting off contact (No Contact) or reducing emotional engagement is feasible.
- Gradually reduce communication and interactions with the narcissist in a safe manner.
- Block their access to your personal life through phone, social media, and mutual friends.
- If full disengagement is not possible (e.g., co-parenting, work), practice emotional detachment and non-reactive responses.
- Seek legal or professional support if required for situations like co-parenting.

What you are going to achieve:

Reducing or cutting off contact helps break the cycle of manipulation and allows you to reclaim your independence. The emotional distance created gives you space to heal and refocus on your own growth.

"I always advise people,

*never 'instantly respond' to
a text message or an email.*

*respond 1 hour,
or a day later"*

Graham McFarland

Action 4:

Seek Professional Support

Steps to Take:

- Consider speaking with a therapist specializing in narcissistic abuse recovery.
- Join support groups (online or in-person) where you can share your experiences and receive validation.
- Work with a life coach to set personal goals and develop a plan for rebuilding self-confidence.
- Consult a legal professional if financial, custody, or workplace concerns arise due to the narcissistic individual's actions.
- Explore self-help books and online resources recommended by experts.

What you are going to achieve:

Professional support offers objective insights and practical coping strategies tailored to your specific situation. It accelerates your healing journey and provides a safe space for emotional processing.

Remember that during this time you are not your best self! Having someone that can help you talk through options objectively is powerful. It also buffers you from the pitfalls from making the wrong decision.

Action 5:

Rebuild Your Self-Esteem and Self-Identity

Steps to Take:

- Engage in self-care activities such as exercise, meditation, and creative hobbies that promote positive self-image.
- Reflect on personal goals, values, and aspirations that were overshadowed by the narcissistic relationship.
- Surround yourself with supportive and uplifting individuals who value you for who you are.
- Develop positive affirmations and practice self-compassion daily.
- Set small, achievable goals to restore confidence and reclaim independence.

What you are going to achieve:

Rebuilding self-esteem allows you to rediscover your authentic self and regain the confidence lost during the abusive relationship. This transformation is key to moving forward and making healthier relationship choices.

Action 6:

Develop Coping Strategies for Emotional Triggers

Steps to Take:

- Identify emotional triggers caused by past narcissistic abuse (e.g., criticism, gas-lighting, rejection).
- Practice grounding techniques such as deep breathing, mindfulness, or journaling.
- Learn to differentiate between healthy conflict and manipulative tactics.
- Develop a "safe response plan" for situations that might evoke past trauma.
- Remind yourself that healing takes time and setbacks are part of the process.

What you are going to achieve:

Having coping mechanisms in place helps you navigate emotional triggers without falling back into old patterns. These strategies build resilience and empower you to handle challenging situations with confidence.

Action 7:

Create a New Vision for Your Future

Steps to Take:

- Define what a healthy, fulfilling life looks like for your post-recovery.
- Set new personal and professional goals based on your values and interests.
- Explore new social circles and activities that align with your authentic self.
- Practice gratitude by acknowledging your progress and growth.
- Stay committed to self-improvement and avoid engaging in toxic relationships.

What you are going to achieve:

Creating a new vision for your future helps you focus on growth and happiness beyond the influence of narcissistic abuse. It empowers you to take control of your life and build fulfilling, meaningful relationships.

Action 8:

Educate Yourself to Prevent Future Toxic Relationships

Steps to Take:

- Learn the early warning signs of narcissistic individuals to avoid repeating patterns.
- Understand the dynamics of healthy vs. toxic relationships.
- Practice healthy communication and assertiveness in new relationships.
- Seek feedback from trusted friends or professionals before entering new partnerships.
- Trust your instincts and prioritize your well-being in all interactions.

What you are going to achieve:

Education is a powerful tool that helps you recognize red flags early and make informed decisions in future relationships. Staying informed empowers you to cultivate healthier and more fulfilling connections.

Final Thoughts:

Moving Toward a Healthier Future

Overcoming the effects of a narcissistic relationship requires courage, self-awareness, and a commitment to personal growth. By following this action plan, individuals can regain their confidence, set healthy boundaries, and build a life free from emotional manipulation.

Taking each step at your own pace and seeking support when needed will pave the way for a brighter, healthier future.

9
INDUSTRY Experts to look out for

Understanding narcissism is crucial for recognizing and addressing its impacts in various aspects of life. Several experts have significantly contributed to this field, offering valuable insights through research, clinical practice, and public education.

Below are some of the leading figures in the study of narcissism, both internationally and within Australia.

Dr. Ramani Durvasula

Dr. Ramani Durvasula is a renowned clinical psychologist, professor, and author specializing in narcissism and narcissistic abuse. She has gained widespread recognition for her ability to demystify complex psychological concepts, making them accessible to a broad audience. Dr. Durvasula's work emphasizes the importance of understanding narcissistic behavior patterns to foster healthier relationships and personal well-being.

Her book, "*It's Not You: Identifying and Healing from Narcissistic People,*" delves into the intricacies of narcissistic personalities and provides practical advice for individuals dealing with narcissists in their personal and professional lives. Through her popular YouTube channel and social media presence as "@DoctorRamani", she offers guidance on recognizing narcissistic traits, setting boundaries, and healing from narcissistic abuse. Watch one every night before you go to sleep.

Dr. Durvasula's expertise has been featured on various media platforms, including the TODAY show and Good Morning America, where she discusses topics related to narcissism and its impact on relationships. Her approachable style and evidence-based insights have made her a trusted resource for those seeking to understand and navigate the challenges associated with narcissistic individuals.

Dr. W. Keith Campbell

Dr. W. Keith Campbell is a prominent social psychologist known for his extensive research on narcissism. As a professor in the Department of Psychology at the University of Georgia, he has authored over 120 peer-reviewed papers and several influential books on the subject.

One of his notable works, "The Narcissism Epidemic: Living in the Age of Entitlement," co-authored with Jean Twenge, explores the rise of narcissistic behavior in modern society and its cultural implications. Dr. Campbell's research delves into various facets of narcissism, including its impact on relationships, self-perception, and societal trends.

His scholarly contributions have been instrumental in advancing the understanding of narcissism as a complex and multifaceted personality trait. Dr. Campbell's work provides valuable insights into how narcissism develops, manifests, and affects individuals and communities.

Dr. Karyl McBride

Dr. Karyl McBride is an American author and licensed marriage and family therapist with over four decades of experience. She specializes in helping individuals recover from the effects of relationships with narcissists, focusing particularly on daughters of narcissistic mothers.

Her seminal book, *"Will I Ever Be Good Enough? Healing the Daughters of Narcissistic Mothers,"* addresses the unique challenges faced by women raised by narcissistic parents. Dr. McBride offers practical guidance for healing and breaking the cycle of narcissistic abuse. She has also developed online workshops and resources to support individuals navigating the complexities of narcissistic relationships.

Dr. McBride's compassionate approach and practical strategies have made her a leading authority in the field of narcissistic abuse recovery. Her work empowers individuals to understand their experiences, heal from past wounds, and build healthier relationships.

Dr. Joshua Miller

Dr. Joshua Miller is a professor of psychology and the director of clinical training at the University of Georgia. His research focuses on the intersection of personality traits and personality disorders, with a particular emphasis on narcissism and psychopathy.

Dr. Miller has contributed to the understanding of narcissism through numerous publications and research studies. His work examines the nuances of narcissistic traits, their assessment, and their implications for interpersonal relationships and mental health.

His scholarly work has been instrumental in refining the conceptualization and measurement of narcissism, providing a deeper understanding of its various dimensions and manifestations.

Nova Gibson

Nova Gibson is an Australian counselor specializing in supporting victims of narcissistic abuse. She emphasizes that narcissism encompasses a spectrum of traits and behaviors, which can have profound effects on those involved with narcissistic individuals. Gibson's work focuses on helping individuals recognize narcissistic patterns, understand their impact, and develop strategies for recovery.

Through her counseling services, Gibson provides a safe and supportive environment for individuals to explore their experiences and work towards healing. Her practical approach and empathetic understanding make her a valuable resource for those affected by narcissistic relationships.

Professor Sam Vaknin

Professor Sam Vaknin is a globally recognized expert in the field of narcissism, psychopathy, and personality disorders. As a professor of clinical psychology at several institutions, including the Southern Federal University (SFU), CIAPS, and SEEU, his research has been instrumental in advancing the understanding of narcissistic personality disorder (NPD) and its impact on individuals and relationships.

Vaknin's work delves deep into the psychological mechanisms of narcissists, their manipulative behaviors, and the devastating effects they can have on victims. His expertise is widely acknowledged, with his insights shaping both academic discourse and public awareness on the subject. His multidisciplinary approach, blending psychology, philosophy, and neuroscience, makes his analyses uniquely comprehensive and thought-provoking.

One of his most influential works, *"Malignant Self-Love: Narcissism Revisited"*, is considered a foundational text for understanding narcissism from both a clinical and personal perspective. First published in 1999 and continuously updated, this book provides an in-depth exploration of narcissistic traits, abusive behaviors, and the underlying psychological constructs that drive narcissists.

Vaknin's insights are drawn from both his academic research and personal experiences, offering readers a rare, inside-out perspective on the disorder. His ability to break down complex psychological theories into accessible language makes this book an essential read for mental health professionals, survivors of narcissistic abuse, and anyone interested in understanding the toxic dynamics of narcissistic relationships.

Beyond his written work, Professor Vaknin is highly active in online education, frequently sharing his expertise through lectures, interviews, and YouTube content. His ability to dissect narcissistic behavior in real-time and explain its implications has made him a valuable resource for those seeking clarity on how to identify and cope with narcissistic individuals.

His contributions to the field continue to be invaluable for those struggling with the emotional and psychological aftermath of narcissistic abuse. For readers looking to deepen their understanding, Malignant Self-Love remains his most well-known work, but his online presence provides an ongoing source of cutting-edge analysis and discussion in the field of personality disorders.

Richard Grannon

Richard Grannon, widely known as the Spartan Life Coach, has gained a strong following for his fresh and practical approach to psychological healing and personal growth. With a background in psychology and neurolinguistic programming (NLP), Grannon specializes in helping individuals recover from narcissistic abuse, toxic relationships, and emotional trauma.

His work is characterized by a no-nonsense, direct style that resonates with those seeking clear guidance on breaking free from destructive patterns. Drawing from both academic research and real-world experience, he empowers people to reclaim their confidence, set boundaries, and rebuild their lives after emotional abuse.

One of Grannon's most impactful works is The Narcissism Recovery Guide, in which he provides structured, actionable advice for identifying and detaching from narcissistic relationships. His approach integrates psychological principles with martial arts philosophy, emphasizing resilience, discipline, and mental toughness.

Unlike traditional self-help authors, Grannon blends psychological education with personal empowerment, making his insights accessible and immediately useful. His ability to communicate complex emotional concepts in an engaging, straightforward manner has made him a favorited among survivors of narcissistic abuse and those struggling with self-doubt.

Beyond his written work, Grannon is best known for his engaging online content, particularly through YouTube and social media, where he offers deep-dive discussions, Q&A sessions, and practical exercises for personal transformation. His unique ability to blend academic psychology with street-smart wisdom has made him a go-to resource for those looking to heal from past trauma and develop emotional resilience.

For readers seeking an insightful and practical guide to overcoming toxic relationships, The Narcissism Recovery Guide is an essential read, while his online courses and video content provide ongoing support and education for anyone on the path to self-discovery and healing.

Dr. Jordan Peterson

Dr. Jordan Peterson, a clinical psychologist and professor of psychology, has gained international recognition for his deep insights into human behavior, personal responsibility, and the structures of meaning that govern our lives.

While much of his work focuses on philosophy, mythology, and self-improvement, he has also provided valuable commentary on narcissism and its impact on individuals and society. Peterson's perspective on narcissism often intersects with his broader discussions on the dangers of ideological possession, entitlement, and the consequences of an unchecked ego.

His ability to connect psychological principles with historical and cultural narratives makes his approach to understanding narcissistic traits unique and thought-provoking.

One of the key areas where Peterson addresses narcissism is in his bestselling books "*12 Rules for Life: An Antidote to Chaos*" and "*Beyond Order: 12 More Rules for Life*". He discusses the importance of humility, self-awareness, and personal accountability as antidotes to narcissistic tendencies.

Peterson often critiques modern cultural trends that encourage self-indulgence and victimhood, warning that these attitudes can lead to a narcissistic worldview where individuals refuse to take responsibility for their actions.

His lectures frequently highlight how narcissistic traits, such as arrogance, deceit, and manipulativeness, can not only damage personal relationships but also erode the foundations of a functional society.

In his online lectures and interviews, Peterson has dissected the psychological underpinnings of narcissistic behavior, particularly in relation to social dominance, power-seeking, and the dangers of pathological leaders. He explores how narcissistic individuals manipulate others through deception and grandiosity, often masking deep insecurity.

Narcissistic Abuse Counseling Service

Brighter Outlook

Based in Australia, Brighter Outlook is a counseling service dedicated to helping individuals recover from narcissistic abuse. The service is recognized as a leading expert in the field within Australia, with clients including clinical psychologists, social workers, medical doctors, and even psychiatrists seeking assistance for themselves.

Brighter Outlook offers specialized support for those struggling to leave abusive relationships, providing tailored counseling services to address the unique challenges associated with narcissistic abuse.

Their comprehensive approach includes individual counseling, support groups, and educational resources designed to empower individuals to break free from abusive dynamics and rebuild their lives. Brighter Outlook's commitment to specialized care has made it a trusted resource for those seeking recovery from narcissistic abuse in Australia.

These experts and organizations have significantly contributed to the understanding of narcissism and the support of individuals affected by narcissistic relationships. Their work offers valuable resources for recognizing narcissistic traits, understanding their impact, and implementing strategies for healing and personal growth.

10

The Power of Your Journey

A cautionary chapter
As you've worked your way through this book, there's been one central theme—understanding narcissism. Learning to recognize manipulation, seeing the red flags, and identifying the toxic behaviors that have shaped your relationships. But now, as we move forward, i need you to pause and take a deep breath because this journey is not about them.

This journey is about you.

Everything you've read, every insight you've gained, and every realization you've had, these aren't weapons to use against the narcissist in your life. This book is not about calling them out, demanding they acknowledge what they've done, or waiting for them to change. That path leads nowhere.

This book is about you taking personal accountability for your life moving forward.

Shifting the focus: from them to you

It's easy to fall into the trap of believing that confronting a narcissist will lead to justice or closure. You may want them to acknowledge the pain they've caused, to admit they were wrong, to apologize for their actions. But let me be brutally honest—that will never happen.

<u>Narcissists do not take responsibility</u>

They do not have the emotional depth to reflect, and they certainly do not see themselves as the villain in your story. If you continue focusing on their behavior, you remain stuck in the same cycle they conditioned you into—a cycle of waiting, hoping, and ultimately feeling disappointed.

But when you shift the focus back to yourself, everything changes. You become the author of your own story.

*"You stop waiting for an apology that will never come.
You stop needing validation from someone incapable
of giving it.
You reclaim your personal power and rewrite
the future ahead of you".*

This is your moment of transformation.

Graham McFarland

Personal power: reclaiming your will and strength

Personal power is not about revenge. It is not about proving a point or making someone else accountable for their actions. It is about owning your journey, healing your wounds, and committing to being the best version of yourself.

Personal power means:
- learning from your past, not being trapped by it.
- holding yourself accountable for your own healing.
- taking action to build the life you deserve.

Right now, you may still feel broken. You may feel like the damage is permanent, like the years lost to a toxic relationship have stolen your ability to trust, love, or dream again. But i promise you—those deep depressive thoughts are not real.

Pain is real, yes. The struggle is real. But the thought that you will never escape it? That is a lie. It's the last whisper of the narcissist's control, the residue of years of gaslighting and manipulation trying to keep you small.

But you are not small.

You are stronger than you know, and the very fact that you are reading this, that you are choosing to understand and grow, is proof of that strength.

Your amazing future is waiting

Right now, your future is unwritten. That's the most beautiful part of this journey—it doesn't matter how much time you lost, how much pain you endured, or how long you stayed in the cycle. None of that defines your future.

What defines your future is what you do now.

Imagine, for a moment, the version of yourself that exists beyond this struggle. Picture the life you never thought possible while under their control.

The version of you who wakes up excited for the day ahead, rather than walking on eggshells.
The version of you who laughs freely, feeling safe in the presence of real, loving relationships.
The version of you who has goals, hobbies, passions, and a sense of adventure again.
The version of you who no longer carries the weight of what was done to them.
That person is waiting for you.

Your future is not defined by the narcissist's presence in your life. It is defined by what you do after them.

Take action

Start becoming the best version of yourself
Healing is not just about letting go—it's about actively moving forward.

Here's how you begin:
Stop analyzing them –
Start understanding yourself, every minute spent analyzing the narcissist is a minute wasted on someone who will never change. Use that

energy to reflect on you. What do you want from life? What makes you happy?

Develop a daily routine

A routine that builds you up physical exercise, reading, learning, self-care—make every day about becoming stronger and healthier. Small habits create massive change over time.

Surround yourself with positivity

Seek out people who uplift you, encourage you, and believe in your potential. Remove toxic influences, whether they are people, places, or even social media that keeps you stuck in the past.

*"The more you educate yourself,
the more unshakable you become"*

Graham McFarland

Pursue what you thought you lost

That hobby you gave up? Pick it up again. That dream you shelved because the narcissist made you feel unworthy. Start chasing it.

Learn and grow every single day

The more you educate yourself, the more unshakable you become. Read about resilience, emotional intelligence, and personal development. Knowledge is power.

Final words: the truth about this journey

This is not easy. There will be days when you feel pulled back into old thoughts, days when the loneliness or grief creeps in. But those days do not define your journey. What defines your journey is that you keep going.

You keep choosing yourself.
You keep moving forward.

The narcissist is irrelevant now. They have no control over your future unless you give it to them. And you won't—because you have something far greater waiting for you.

A life that is yours.
A future that is limitless.

A version of yourself that is stronger than you ever imagined. Your past may have been written by manipulation and pain, but your future? That's yours to create. And I can't wait to see who you become.

11

Why I wrote this book

Educating myself about narcissistic abuse and understanding its deep impact has been a trans-formative journey. Through years of self-reflection, research, and personal growth, I have not only rebuilt my self-esteem but also developed a keen sense of character assessment—allowing me to recognize healthy relationships and set strong boundaries.

The irony of this journey is that it ultimately led me to a truly remarkable woman, someone who understands my experiences because she, too, has been a victim of narcissistic abuse. Together, we have supported each other through the healing process, learning to navigate trust and love in ways we never thought possible.

We have both witnessed our narcissistic ex's, and to our amazement that experience is not as familiar as we first thought. Meeting a new narcissist was still raw and unbelievable. Even after so many years, these people still are oblivious that they are this way. They are unaware that we have called them out, and we just don't react or care anymore.

**It is also my belief,
They cannot be changed.**

Its like their bodies are just vessels for these narcissistic characters. But to be honest, these days I just stay clear of these people. I know what to look out for, these "Red Flags"

She has been my rock, and it was her unwavering belief in the importance of raising awareness about female narcissists that inspired me to write this book. Her encouragement and shared understanding have shown me that healing is not only possible but that it can lead to something truly meaningful—a future built on mutual respect, empathy, and strength.

So yes, Alexia is the inspiration of this book. We have debated narcissism for hours and hours, we have watched YouTube videos together, read books sharing our learning and listened to many podcasts together. We share how we were collectively affected and the sharing of solutions to how to overcome a narcissist's strong hold.

It was her that got me started down this path of writing this book.

Thankyou
Alexia!

Yes, Women Can Be Narcissists Too

One of my favorite books

"*The New Science of Narcissism:*
Understanding One of the Greatest Psychological Challenges of Our Time—and What You Can Do About It"
by W. Keith Campbell:

Here is a summary of his work by chapter:

1: Defining Narcissism

This introduces the concept of narcissism, emphasizing its core elements: self-importance, entitlement, and antagonism. Campbell distinguishes between grandiose and vulnerable narcissism, explaining that while grandiose narcissists are outgoing and confident, vulnerable narcissists are introverted and insecure. He also discusses the development of the Trifurcated Model of Narcissism, which integrates both forms to provide a comprehensive understanding.

2: The Roots of Narcissism

In this chapter, Campbell explores the origins of narcissistic traits, examining both genetic predispositions and environmental influences. He delves into how parenting styles, early childhood experiences, and societal factors contribute to the development of narcissism. The also discusses the role of culture and media in shaping narcissistic behaviors.

3: Measuring Narcissism

Campbell discusses the various methods used to assess narcissism, including self-report questionnaires and observational techniques. He evaluates the strengths and limitations of these tools and emphasizes the importance of context when interpreting results. The also introduces the Narcissistic Personality Inventory (NPI) and other scales commonly used in research.

4: Narcissism in Relationships

This examines how narcissism impacts interpersonal relationships. Campbell explains that while narcissists may initially appear charming and attractive, their self-centred behaviors often lead to conflicts and dissatisfaction over time. He provides insights into the dynamics of relationships involving narcissists and offers advice on managing such interactions.

5: Narcissism in the Workplace
Campbell explores the influence of narcissism in professional settings. He discusses how narcissistic traits can both aid and hinder career advancement, noting that while confidence and assertiveness may lead to leadership positions, lack of empathy and exploitative behaviours can result in workplace conflicts and ethical issues.

6: Cultural Reflections of Narcissism
This delves into the portrayal of narcissism in culture and media. Campbell analyses how societal values and technological advancements, particularly social media, have contributed to the rise of narcissistic behaviours. He also discusses the concept of a "narcissism epidemic" and evaluates evidence supporting this idea.

7: The Benefits and Costs of Narcissism
Campbell provides a balanced view of narcissism, acknowledging that certain narcissistic traits can be advantageous in specific contexts, such as leadership and performance arts. However, he also highlights the potential costs, including relationship issues, mental health challenges, and societal impacts.

8: Managing and Mitigating Narcissism
In the final chapter, Campbell offers strategies for individuals to manage their own narcissistic tendencies and to cope with narcissism in others. He emphasizes the importance of self-awareness, empathy development, and setting healthy boundaries. The also discusses therapeutic approaches for addressing narcissistic personality disorder.

Final overview of his book!
"The New Science of Narcissism" provides a comprehensive exploration of narcissism, integrating research findings with practical insights. Campbell effectively distinguishes between grandiose and vulnerable forms, examines their origins and manifestations, and offers guidance on managing narcissism in various aspects of life. The book serves as a valuable resource for understanding this complex personality trait and its implications in contemporary society.

Top Books About NARCISSISM

"**It's Not You:**
Identifying and Healing from Narcissistic People" by Ramani Durvasula

In this insightful guide, Dr. Durvasula helps readers recognize narcissistic behaviors in others and provides strategies for healing from the associated emotional harm. She emphasizes the importance of understanding narcissism's impact on personal well-being and offers practical advice for recovery.

"**The Covert Passive-Aggressive Narcissist:**
Recognizing the Traits and Finding Healing After Hidden Emotional and Psychological Abuse"
by Debbie Mirza

Debbie Mirza delves into the subtle and often unnoticed behaviors of covert narcissists. She provides tools to identify these hidden traits and offers guidance on healing from the psychological abuse they inflict.

"**The Narcissistic Family:**
Diagnosis and Treatment"
by Stephanie Donaldson-Pressman and Robert M. Pressman

This book explores the dynamics of families affected by narcissism, focusing on how such environments impact children. The authors provide therapeutic approaches for clinicians and practical advice for individuals seeking to understand and heal from these family dynamics.

"**The Wizard of Oz and Other Narcissists:**
Coping with the One-Way Relationship in Work, Love, and Family"
by Eleanor D. Payson

Eleanor Payson uses the metaphor of "The Wizard of Oz" to illustrate narcissistic behaviour patterns. She offers strategies for recognizing and managing relationships with narcissists in various aspects of life

"**Disarming the Narcissist:**
Surviving and Thriving with the Self-Absorbed"
by Wendy T. Behary

Wendy Behary combines clinical expertise with practical advice to help readers navigate relationships with narcissists. She emphasizes the importance of setting boundaries and developing empathy to manage interactions effectively.

"The Culture of Narcissism:
American Life in an Age of Diminishing Expectations" by Christopher Lasch
Christopher Lasch provides a cultural critique, arguing that post-World War II America has fostered a personality type consistent with clinical definitions of narcissism. He examines the societal factors contributing to this cultural shift.

"Rethinking Narcissism:
The Secret to Recognizing and Coping with Narcissists" by Dr. Craig Malkin
Dr. Malkin presents a nuanced view of narcissism, suggesting that a certain degree of self-enhancement can be healthy. He introduces the concept of a narcissism spectrum and offers guidance on managing relationships with individuals across this continuum.

"Will I Ever Be Good Enough?
Healing the Daughters of Narcissistic Mothers"
by Karyl McBride
Karyl McBride focuses on the unique challenges faced by daughters of narcissistic mothers. She provides a recovery program to help these women heal and develop a healthy sense of self.

"The New Science of Narcissism:
Understanding One of the Greatest Psychological Challenges of Our Time—and What You Can Do About It"
by W. Keith Campbell
Dr. Campbell offers an in-depth exploration of narcissism, integrating recent research findings. He discusses various forms of narcissism and provides insights into dealing with narcissistic individuals.

"Malignant Self-Love:
Narcissism Revisited"
by Sam Vaknin
Sam Vaknin provides a comprehensive analysis of narcissistic personality disorder from the perspective of someone diagnosed with the condition. He delves into the intricacies of narcissistic behavior and its impact on relationships.

**"The Narcissism Epidemic:
Living in the Age of Entitlement"
by Jean M. Twenge and W. Keith Campbell**

This book examines the rise of narcissistic behaviour in modern society, exploring its causes and consequences. The authors discuss cultural factors contributing to increased narcissism and offer suggestions for mitigating its effects.

"Will I Ever Be Free of You?
How to Navigate a High-Conflict Divorce from a Narcissist and Heal Your Family"
by Karyl McBride
Karyl McBride provides guidance for individuals going through a divorce with a narcissistic partner. She offers strategies to protect oneself and one's children during the process and to heal afterward.

"The Wizard of Oz and Other Narcissists:
Coping with the One-Way Relationship in Work, Love, and Family"
by Eleanor D. Payson
Eleanor Payson uses the metaphor of "The Wizard of Oz" to illustrate narcissistic behaviour patterns. She offers strategies for recognizing and managing relationships with narcissists in various aspects of life.

"The Covert Passive-Aggressive Narcissist:
Recognizing the Traits and Finding Healing After Hidden Emotional and Psychological Abuse"
by Debbie Mirza
Debbie Mirza delves into the subtle and often unnoticed behaviours of covert narcissists. She provides tools to identify these hidden traits and offers guidance on healing from the psychological abuse they inflict.

"Disarming the Narcissist:
Surviving and Thriving with the Self-Absorbed"
by Wendy T. Behary
Wendy Behary combines clinical expertise with practical advice to help readers navigate relationships with narcissists. She emphasizes the importance of setting boundaries and developing empathy to manage interactions effectively.

"The Culture of Narcissism:
American Life in an Age of Diminishing Expectations"
by Christopher Lasch
Christopher Lasch provides a cultural critique, arguing that post-World War II America has fostered a personality type consistent with clinical definitions of narcissism. He examines the societal factors contributing to this cultural shift.

"Will I Ever Be Good Enough?
Healing the Daughters of Narcissistic Mothers"
by Karyl McBride

Karyl McBride focuses on the unique challenges faced by daughters of narcissistic mothers. She provides a recovery program to help these women heal and develop a healthy sense of self.

"The New Science of Narcissism:
Understanding One of the Greatest Psychological Challenges of Our Time—
and What You Can Do About It"
by W. Keith Campbell
Dr. Campbell offers an in-depth exploration of narcissism, integrating recent research findings

How To Kill A Narcissist:
Debunking The Myth Of Narcissism And Recovering From Narcissistic Abuse
by JH Simon
'How To Kill A Narcissist' is a book with two aims:
1. To reveal the rotten core of the narcissistic personality so you can see it clearly
2. To present you with an inside-out strategy for healing, recovery and freedom

Whether you are dealing with narcissistic parents, husbands, wives, friends, bosses or colleagues, the same philosophy will apply.

You will gain tools for disarming a narcissist i.e. starving them of their narcissistic supply

*"you might find some "writers"
don't resonate well with you.
by reading a wider range
of resources
you start to comprehend
a deeper understanding"*

Graham McFarland